EARTH'S NATURAL DISASTERS

VOLATILE VOLCANOES

Jane Katirgis and Michele Ingber Drohan

Enslow Publishing
101 W. 23rd Street
Suite 240
New York, NY 10011
USA

enslow.com

Words to Know

lava—Magma that reaches the surface of the earth.

magma—Hot, liquid rock.

phreatic—A type of eruption in which steam is created by water hitting magma.

Plinian—A type of eruption that creates a huge mushroom cloud.

rift zone—An area where two plates have broken apart and made a crack in the earth's crust.

seismometer—An instrument used to measure movement in the earth.

Strombolian—A violent volcanic eruption in which lava and rocks are shot high into the air.

subduction zone—An area where two plates hit and one forces the other into the mantle, forming a crack.

volcanic eruption—Magma coming through a crack in the Earth's crust.

volcanologist—A person who studies volcanoes.

Contents

Words to Know 2

1 The Layers of the Earth 5

2 Volcano Science 6

3 Volcanoes Around the World 12

4 A Volcano Erupts 16

5 Predicting an Eruption 22

6 Volcanoes and the Earth 28

Learn More 30

Index 31

The earth's layers include the crust, the mantle, and the core.

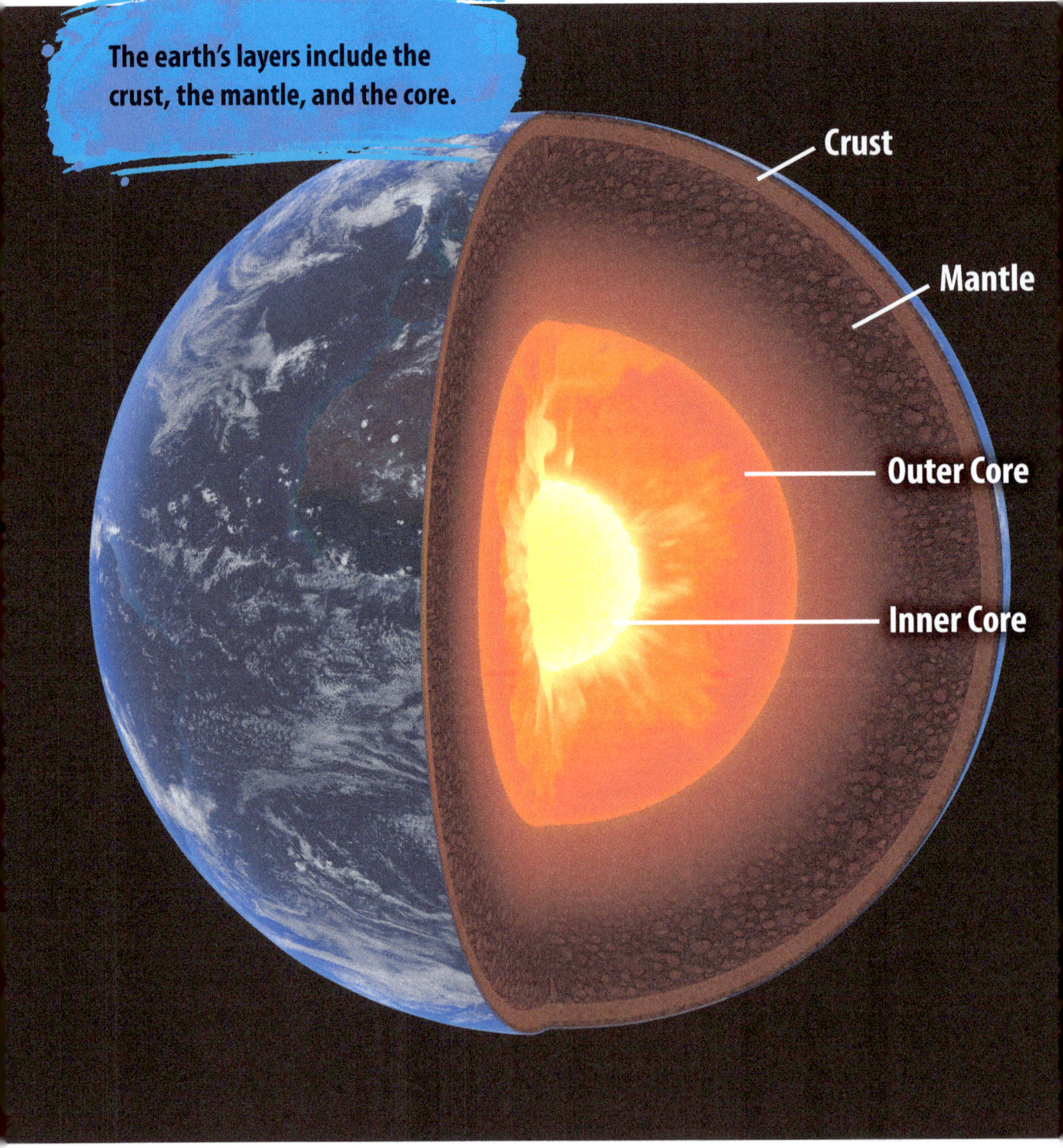

1

THE LAYERS OF THE EARTH

The earth has three layers of rock. The top layer is called the crust. The crust is solid rock and covers the whole surface of the earth. We live on the crust. The middle layer is called the mantle. The mantle is solid rock filled with pockets of liquid rock called **magma**. The center of the earth is called the core. The core is part magma and part solid rock. It is the earth's hottest place. The distance from the earth's crust to the center of the core is about 4,000 miles (6,437 km).

2

Volcano Science

The earth's crust is broken into pieces called plates. The plates only move about 2 inches (5 cm) every year. A volcano forms when a crack opens in the crust either between plates or in the middle of them. This can happen when the plates break apart, causing a **rift zone**. It can also happen when plates bump into each other. One plate forces the other down into the mantle, forming a **subduction zone**. Magma can then get through the crust and cause a **volcanic eruption**. When magma reaches the earth's surface, it is called **lava**.

THREE TYPES OF PLATE BOUNDARIES

Divergent plate boundary

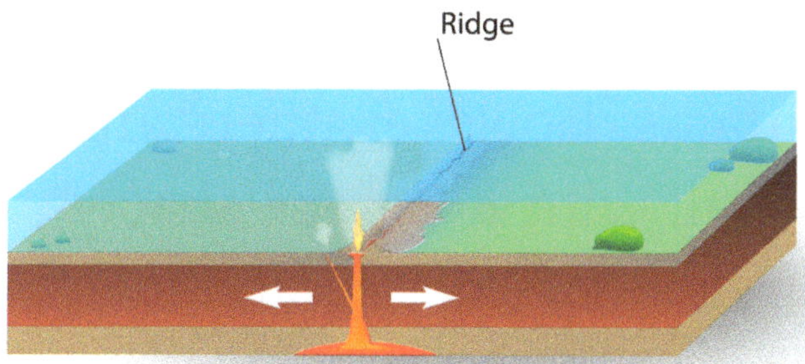

Transform plate boundary

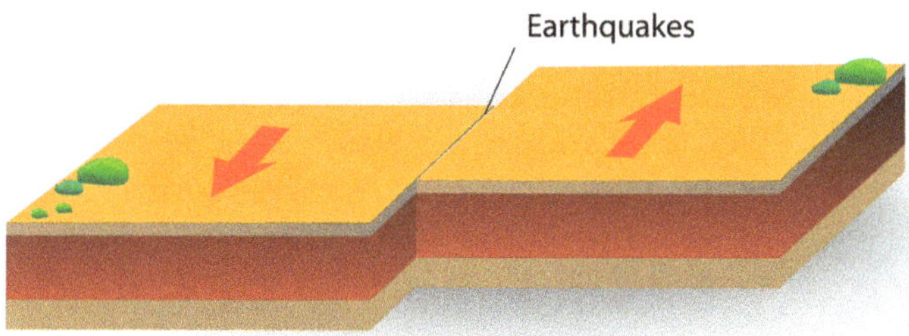

Convergent plate boundary

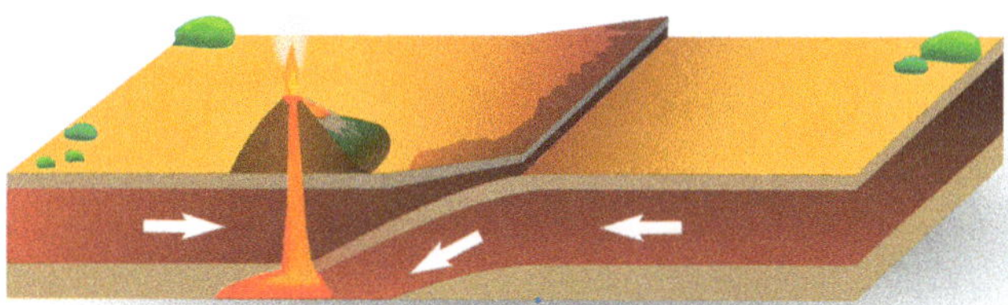

Once a crack in the earth's crust has formed, magma can get through.

Types of Volcanoes

Many people think that volcanoes always look like mountains. However, there are four kinds of volcanoes, all with different shapes. Sometimes volcanoes do look like mountains. These form when magma comes out of the earth's crust and cools into hard rock. Over time, this rock builds

A Shield Volcano in Hawaii

Kilauea may be the most active volcano on earth. It is one of five volcanoes that form the island of Hawaii. It has been erupting since 1983! Its name means "much spreading." This is because of the lava that often flows out of it and spreads over the land.

The lava flowing from this volcano covers the land around it. The area, 48 square miles (124 km^2), is the size of more than 20,000 football fields.

The Kilauea volcano in Hawaii has been erupting for decades.

Types of Volcanoes

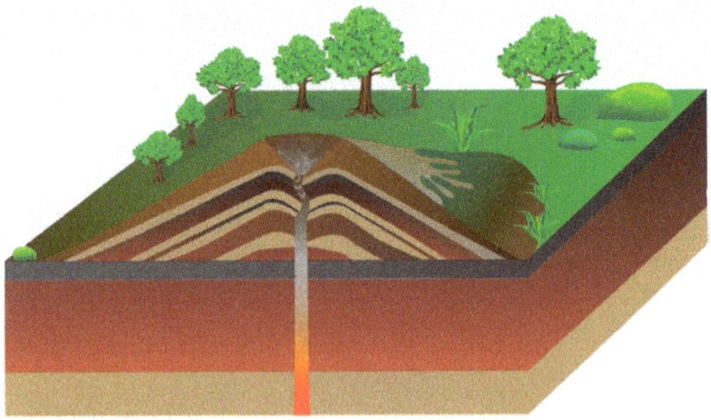

lava dome volcano

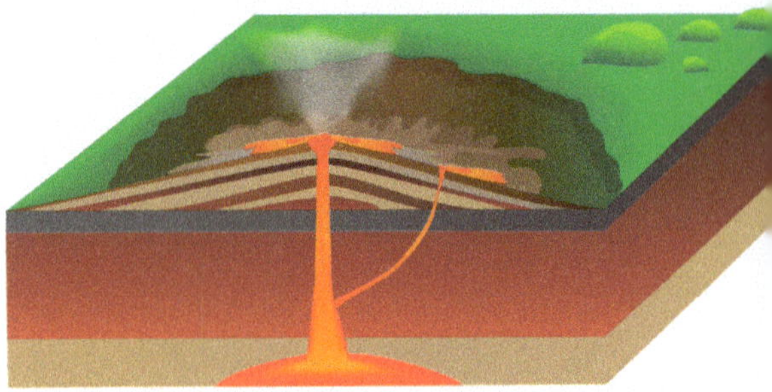

shield volcano

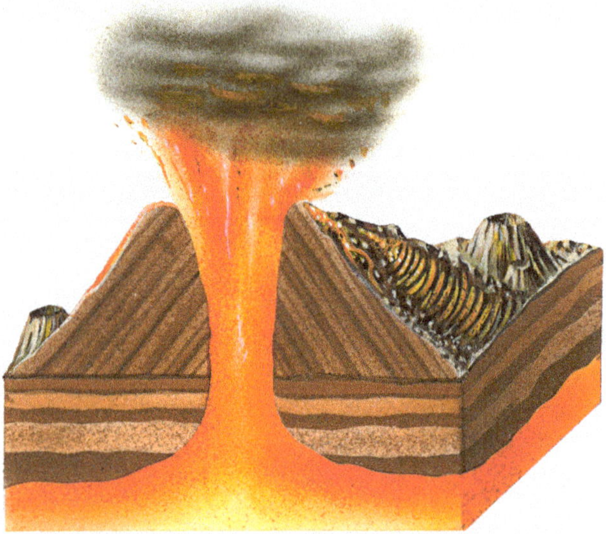

cinder-cone

stratovolcano

into the shape of a mountain. Mount St. Helens in Washington State, Mount Fuji in Japan, and Mount Vesuvius in Italy were all made this way. They are called stratovolcanoes. The three other types of volcanoes are called shield, cinder-cone, and dome volcanoes. They are named for their shapes.

3

Volcanoes Around the World

Where on earth can you find a volcano? Volcanoes are found all over the world. Many are located in the countries around the Pacific Ocean. Scientists call this area the Ring of Fire. All the volcanoes in this area are made by subduction zones. Most of these volcanoes are dormant. This means they haven't erupted in a long time.

The Mid-Atlantic Rift Zone is found in the middle of the Atlantic Ocean. It has the most active

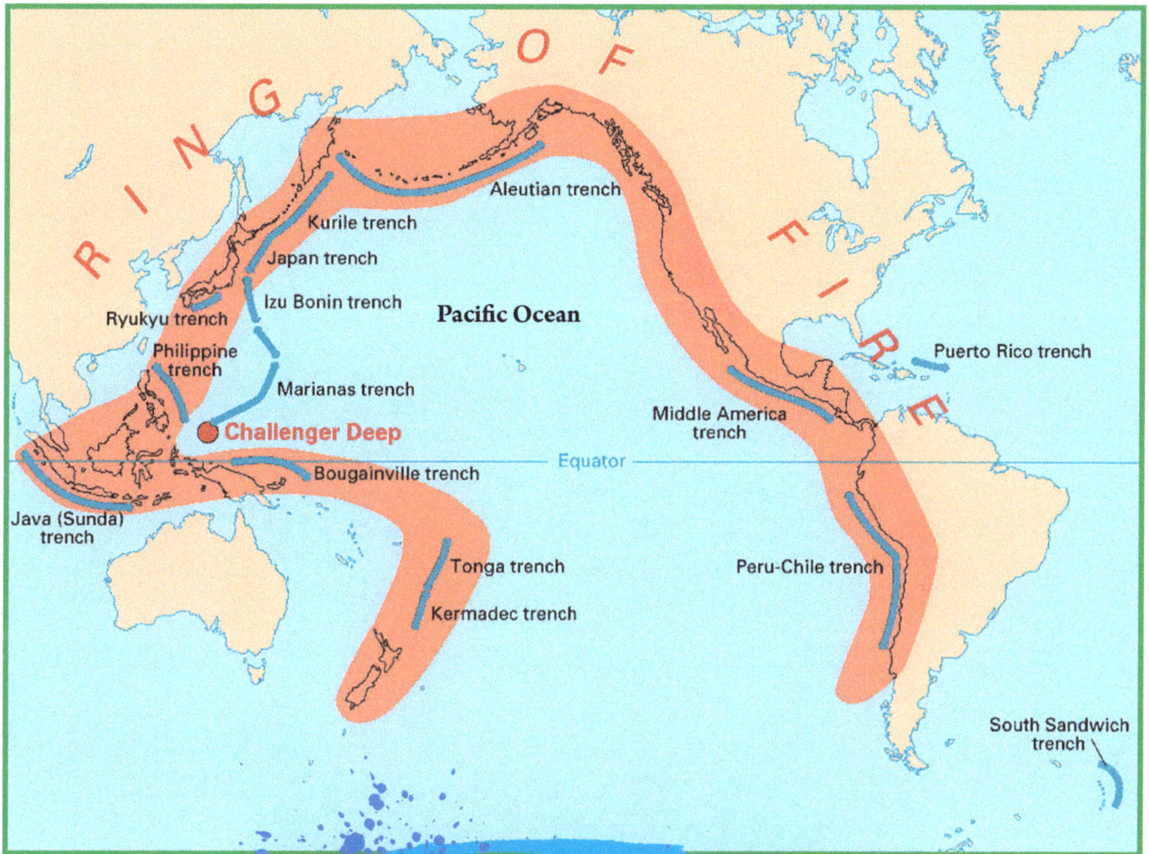

The Ring of Fire is a hot spot of volcanoes around the Pacific Ocean.

Hawaii has a lot of volcanoes, and Mauna Loa is its largest.

volcanoes in the world. This means they erupt a lot. You can't see them because they are under the ocean!

Hot Spots

Volcanoes usually form where two plates meet. However, sometimes a volcano forms in the middle of a plate. This is called a hot spot. Scientists don't know why this happens, but they do know how it happens. A hot spot occurs where magma melts through the plate. This forms a volcano. Scientists believe that this is how volcanoes on Hawaii were made. Mauna Loa is the largest of the many volcanoes on Hawaii. It is 70 miles (113 km) long and 30,000 feet (9,144 m) high.

4

A Volcano Erupts

A volcano can erupt in different ways. In a Hawaiian-type eruption, lava flows out freely like hot fudge on ice cream. In a **phreatic** eruption, steam, created by water touching the magma inside a volcano, is released. It looks like steam from a boiling kettle. Phreatic eruptions usually occur under the ocean.

Other kinds of eruptions happen on land. One is called a **Plinian** eruption, also known as a Vesuvian eruption. It looks like a big mushroom cloud, and it

A Plinian eruption occurs on Popocatepetl, a volcano in Mexico.

Ice and Fire

In August 2014, a string of earthquakes struck Iceland. The Bardarbunga volcano, a stratovolcano, began erupting and has not stopped. The volcano sits under the ice cap of a glacier on this island. Although it has not released much ash, it has been spewing lava and giving off toxic sulfur dioxide gas.

was the kind of eruption that destroyed the Roman city of Pompeii in AD 79. The most violent kind of eruption is called a **Strombolian** eruption. When this happens, thick lava blocks gases from getting out of the top of the volcano. When enough gas builds up, it shoots the hot rock and lava high into the air.

This Strombolian eruption in Italy demonstrates how the lava sprays out with force from the volcano.

A volcanic eruption from Soufriere Hills has caused devastation to the local area.

Volcano Rescue

A volcano erupting near a town or a city is very dangerous. Gases damage the air. Clouds of hot ash can move as fast as 60 miles per hour (97 km/h). The first thing to do if there is an eruption is to get to a safe place. Hot, flowing lava will destroy everything in its path. Rescuers try to stop the flow of lava to save people's homes. They spray the lava with water from fire hoses to cool it. When lava cools, it slows down and then stops. However, it can take a long time to stop a lava flow. Sometimes a volcano erupts for many months or even years. A volcano on an island in the Caribbean Sea called Soufriere Hills has been erupting since 1995. Thousands of people have been forced to leave the island.

5

Predicting an Eruption

Is there a way to know when a volcano is going to erupt? If so, it could save lives. **Volcanologists** are people who study volcanoes. They use special instruments to try to predict when a volcano will erupt. One instrument is called a **seismometer**. It is used to measure movement in the ground.

Seismometers

When magma pushes through a crack in the earth's crust, the ground near the volcano shifts. If the

Scientists who study volcanoes are called volcanologists.

Alaskan Volcano Erupts

Scientists had been watching Mount Redoubt in Alaska. In February 2009, members of the Alaskan Volcano Observatory flew over the volcano. They saw a hole in the glacier as big as a football field. Steam was pouring out of the hole and melting the snow and ice around it. They knew things were changing inside the volcano. On March 22, 2009, the glacier-topped peak erupted. It blew ash into the air as high as 9 miles (14 km)!

seismometer says that the ground is moving a lot, the volcanologist knows that the volcano may erupt at any time. Even with these instruments, scientists can't be exactly sure when a volcano will erupt, but they still try. The more exact they can be, the more people they can save.

Mount Redoubt in Alaska erupted in 2009, blowing ash into the air.

Scientists had been watching Mount St. Helens and thought it was ready to erupt. In 1980, they were proven right as it blasted ash into the air.

Mount St. Helens

In 1978, volcanologists predicted that Mount St. Helens would erupt some time in the next ten years. They were right. Mount St. Helens erupted in 1980. Many people were saved because they were told the volcano would erupt. They left before it happened. Fifty-seven people who did not leave were killed by the blast. Homes, highways, and forests were destroyed. It was the worst eruption in the history of the United States. In 1982, the area became the Mount St. Helens National Volcanic Monument. Many people visit it every year to learn about volcanoes.

6

Volcanoes and the Earth

Volcanoes are dangerous, but they also give the earth many good things. The heat inside a volcano can be used to make electricity. Lava rock is used to make new roads. Diamonds and metals, such as copper and tin, are usually found near volcanoes. The ash from volcanoes is good for the earth's soil. The ash makes the soil rich. Rich soil is good for growing plants, including crops for food. Soon after a volcanic eruption, animals return and plants grow again.

Lots of lush green growth has sprouted up next to the Arenal volcano in Costa Rica.

Learn More

Books

Greenwood, Rosie. ***I Wonder Why Volcanoes Blow Their Tops and Other Questions About Natural Disasters.*** New York: Kingfisher, 2013.

Jackson, Tom. ***Magic School Bus Presents: Volcanoes & Earthquakes.*** New York: Scholastic, 2014.

Rustad, Martha. ***Volcanoes.*** North Mankato, Minn.: Capstone Press, 2013.

Web Sites

discoverykids.com/games/volcano-explorer/

Read about types of volcanoes, see virtual volcanoes, and build your own volcano.

kids.nationalgeographic.com/explore/science/volcano/

Facts about volcanoes.

INDEX

A

Alaskan Volcano Observatory, 24
ash, 18, 21, 24, 28

B

Bardarbunga, 18

C

cinder-cones, 11
crust, 5, 6, 8, 22

D

dome volcanoes, 11
dormant volcanoes, 12

F

Fuji, Mount, 11

H

Hawaii, 8, 15
Hawaiian-type eruptions, 16
hot spots, 15

I

Iceland, 18

L

lava, 6, 8, 16, 18, 21, 28

M

magma, 5, 6, 8, 15, 16, 22
mantle, 5, 6
Mauna Loa, 15

P

phreatic eruptions, 16
plates, 6, 15
Plinian eruptions, 16
predicting eruptions, 22

R

Redoubt, Mount, 24
rift zones, 6, 12
Ring of Fire, 12

S

St. Helens, Mount, 11, 27
seismometers, 22, 24
shield volcanoes, 8, 11
stratovolcanoes, 11, 18
Strombolian eruptions, 18
subduction zones, 6, 12

V

Vesuvius, Mount, 11
volcanic eruptions, 6, 28
volcanologists, 22, 24, 27

Published in 2016 by Enslow Publishing, LLC.
101 W. 23rd Street, Suite 240, New York, NY 10011

Library of Congress Cataloging-in-Publication Data
Katirgis, Jane, author.
Volatile volcanoes / Jane Katirgis and Michele Ingber Drohan.
pages cm. — (Earth's natural disasters)
Summary: "Discusses the science behind volcanoes and what to do to stay safe from them"— Provided by publisher.
Audience: 8+
Audience: Grades 4 to 6
Includes bibliographical references and index.
ISBN 978-0-7660-6803-2 (library binding)
ISBN 978-0-7660-6801-8 (pbk.)
ISBN 978-0-7660-6802-5 (6-pack)
I. Drohan, Michele Ingber, author. II. Title.
QE521.3.K38 2015
551.21—dc23
2015008024

Printed in the United States of America

To Our Readers: We have done our best to make sure all Web sites in this book were active and appropriate when we went to press. However, the author and the publisher have no control over and assume no liability for the material available on those Web sites or on any Web sites they may link to. Any comments or suggestions can be sent by e-mail to customerservice@enslow.com.

Photo Credits: Al Grillo/AP Images, p. 25; Bernhard Edmaier/LOOK-foto/Look/Getty Images, p. 19; Bocxe Wesley/Science Source/Getty Images, p. 17; ByrneImagery/Shutterstock.com, p. 9; Designua/Shutterstock.com, pp. 7, 10 (lava dome, shield volcano); Dorling Kindersley/Getty Images, p. 10 (cinder-cone, stratovolcano); EpicStockMedia/Shutterstock.com (chapter openers and back matter backgrounds); Jack Smith/AP Images, p. 25; Jamie Farrant/Digital Vision Vectors (caption boxes); Joe Carini/Perspectives/Getty Images, p. 14; Johan Swanepoel/Shutterstock.com, p. 4; Mike Lyvers/Moment Open/Getty Images, p. 20; Nickolay Stanev/Shutterstock.com, p. 29; Pablo Hidalgo - Fotos593/Shutterstock.com, p. 1; Photo Researchers/Science SourceGetty Images, p. 23; traffic_analyzer/Digital Vision Vectors/Getty Images (page folios); U.S. Geological Survey Department of the Interior/USGS/Reston, VA, p.13.

Cover Credits: Pablo Hidalgo - Fotos593/Shutterstock.com (volcano); EpicStockMedia/Shutterstock.com (background); traffic_analyzer/Digital Vision Vectors/Getty Images (series icon).